Congressional
Research
Service

Medicare: Part B Premiums

Patricia A. Davis
Specialist in Health Care Financing

June 11, 2013

Congressional Research Service

7-5700

www.crs.gov

R40082

CRS Report for Congress

Prepared for Members and Committees of Congress

Summary

Medicare is a federal insurance program that pays for covered health care services of most individuals aged 65 and over and certain disabled persons. In 2013, the program is expected to cover 52 million persons (43 million aged and 9 million disabled) at a total cost of $594 billion. Most individuals (or their spouses) who are 65 and older, and have worked in covered employment and paid Medicare payroll taxes for 40 quarters receive premium-free Medicare Part A (Hospital Insurance). Those entitled to Medicare Part A (regardless of whether they are eligible for premium-free Part A), have the option of enrolling in Part B, which covers such things as physician and outpatient services and medical equipment.

Beneficiaries have a seven-month initial enrollment period, but those who enroll in Part B after their initial enrollment period and/or reenroll after a termination of coverage may be subject to a "delayed enrollment penalty" which is equal to a 10% surcharge for each 12 months of delay in enrollment and/or reenrollment. Under certain conditions, select beneficiaries are exempt from the delayed enrollment penalty; these include working individuals (and their spouses) with group coverage, some military retirees, and some international volunteers.

While Part A is financed primarily by payroll taxes paid by current workers, Part B is financed through a combination of beneficiary premiums and federal general revenues. The standard Part B premiums are set to cover 25% of projected per capita Part B program costs for the aged, with federal general revenues accounting for the remaining amount. In general, if projected Part B costs increase or decrease, the premium rises or falls proportionately.

Most Part B participants must pay monthly premiums, which do not vary with a beneficiary's age, health status or place of residence. However, since 2007, higher-income enrollees pay higher premiums to cover a higher percentage of Part B costs. Premiums of those receiving benefits through Social Security are deducted from their monthly payments. Additionally, certain low-income beneficiaries may qualify for Medicare cost-sharing and/or premium assistance from Medicaid through a Medicare Savings Program. The Social Security Act includes a provision that holds most Social Security beneficiaries harmless for increases in the Medicare Part B premium; affected beneficiaries' Part B premiums are reduced to ensure that their Social Security checks do not decline from one year to the next.

Each year, the Centers for Medicare & Medicaid Services (CMS) determines the Medicare Part B premiums for the following year. The standard monthly Part B premium for 2013 is $104.90. Higher-income beneficiaries, currently defined as those with incomes over $85,000 a year, or couples with incomes over $170,000 per year, pay $146.90, $209.80, $272.70, or $335.70 per month, depending on their income levels.

Current issues related to the Part B premium that may come before Congress include the amount of the premium and the rate of increase in recent years (and the potential net impact on Social Security benefits), modifications to the late enrollment penalty, and possible increases in Medicare premiums as a means to reduce federal spending and deficits.

Contents

Figures

Tables

Appendixes

Contacts

Introduction

Medicare is a federal insurance program that pays for covered health care services of most individuals aged 65 and over and certain disabled persons. Medicare serves approximately one in six Americans and virtually all of the population aged 65 and over. In calendar year (CY)2013, the program is expected to cover 52 million persons (43 million aged and 9 million disabled) at a total cost of $594 billion, accounting for approximately 3.6% of GDP.[1] The Medicare program is administered by the Centers for Medicare & Medicaid Services (CMS).

Medicare consists of four parts—Parts A through D. Part A covers hospital services, skilled nursing facility services, home health visits, and hospice services. Part B covers a broad range of medical services and supplies, including physician services, laboratory services, durable medical equipment, and outpatient hospital services. Enrollment in Part B is voluntary, however most beneficiaries (about 93%) with Part A also enroll in Part B. Part C provides private plan options, such as managed care, for beneficiaries who are enrolled in both Parts A and B. Part D provides optional outpatient prescription drug coverage.[2]

Each part of Medicare is funded differently.[3] Part A is financed primarily through payroll taxes imposed on current workers (2.9% of earnings, shared equally between employers and workers) which is credited to the Hospital Insurance (HI) Trust Fund, and beneficiaries generally do not pay premiums for Part A. In 2013, total Part A expenditures are expected to reach $271 billion representing about 46% of program costs. Parts B and D, the voluntary portions, are funded through the Supplementary Medical Insurance (SMI) Trust Fund which is financed primarily by general revenues (transfers from the Treasury) and premiums paid by enrollees. In 2013, about $2.7 billion in fees on manufacturers and importers of brand-name prescription drugs will also be used to supplement the SMI trust fund.[4] In 2013, Part B expenditures are expected to reach about $251 billion and Part D expenditures, about $72 billion, representing 42% and 12% of program costs respectively. (Part C is financed proportionately through the HI and SMI Trust Funds.)

Part B beneficiary premiums are set at a rate each year equal to 25% of expected per capita Part B program costs for the aged for the year.[5] In 2013, most beneficiaries pay the standard monthly Part B premium of $104.90.[6] Higher-income enrollees pay higher premiums set to cover a higher percentage of Part B costs,[7] while those with low incomes may qualify for premium assistance

---

[1] Estimates from the 2013 Annual Report of the Boards of Trustees of the Federal Hospital Insurance and Federal Supplementary Medical Insurance Trust Funds, http://www.cms.gov/Research-Statistics-Data-and-Systems/Statistics-Trends-and-Reports/ReportsTrustFunds/Downloads/TR2013.pdf.

[2] For additional information on the Medicare program, see CRS Report R40425, *Medicare Primer*, coordinated by Patricia A. Davis and Scott R. Talaga.

[3] See CRS Report R41436, *Medicare Financing*, by Patricia A. Davis.

[4] For additional information see archived CRS Report R41128, *Health-Related Revenue Provisions in the Patient Protection and Affordable Care Act (ACA)*, by Janemarie Mulvey.

[5] Beneficiary premiums cover approximately 12.1% of the costs of "traditional" Medicare (Parts A and B combined), 11.4% from Part B premiums, and 0.7% from voluntary Part A premiums. See **Appendix D** for information on Part A premiums.

[6] Centers for Medicare & Medicaid Services, "Medicare Program: Medicare Part B Monthly Actuarial Rates, Premium Rate, and Annual Deductible Beginning January 1, 2013," 77 *Federal Register* 69850-69859, November 21, 2012, http://www.gpo.gov/fdsys/pkg/FR-2012-11-21/pdf/2012-28275.pdf.

[7] Depending on their level of income, beneficiaries subject to the income-related monthly adjustment pay a total monthly premium of 35%, 50%, 65%, or 80% of expected per capita Part B costs for the aged. See "Income-Related (continued...)

---

through one of several Medicare Savings Programs administered by Medicaid. Individuals who receive Social Security or Railroad Retirement Board retirement or disability benefits have their Part B premiums automatically deducted from their benefit checks. Part B premiums are generally announced in the fall prior to the year that they are in effect (for example, the 2013 Part B premiums were announced in November 2012).[8]

In addition to premiums, Part B beneficiaries must also pay other out-of-pocket costs when they use services. The annual deductible for Part B services is $147 in 2013. After the annual deductible is met, beneficiaries are responsible for coinsurance costs, which are generally 20% of Medicare-approved Part B expenses.

This report provides an overview of Medicare Part B premiums, including information on: Part B eligibility and enrollment; late enrollment penalties; collection of premiums; determination of annual premium amounts; premiums for high-income enrollees; premium assistance for low-income enrollees; protections for Social Security recipients from rising Part B premiums; and, historical Medicare Part B premium trends. This report also provides a summary of various premium related issues that may be of interest to Congress. Specific Medicare and Social Security publications and other resources for beneficiaries, and those who provide assistance to them, are cited where appropriate.

Medicare Part B Eligibility and Enrollment

An individual (or the spouse of an individual) who has worked in covered employment and paid Medicare payroll taxes for 40 quarters is entitled to receive premium-free Medicare Part A benefits upon turning 65. Those who have paid in for fewer than 40 quarters, may enroll in Medicare Part A by paying a premium.[9] All persons entitled to Part A (regardless of whether they are eligible for premium-free Part A) are also entitled to enroll in Part B. An aged person not entitled to Part A may enroll in Part B if he or she is age 65 or over and either a U.S. citizen, or an alien lawfully admitted for permanent residence, who has resided in the United States continuously for the immediately preceding five years.

Those who are receiving Social Security or Railroad Retirement Board (RRB) benefits are automatically enrolled in Medicare, and coverage begins the first day of the month they turn 65.[10] These individuals will receive a Medicare card and a "Welcome to Medicare" package about three months before their 65th birthday.[11] Those who are automatically enrolled in Medicare Part

---

(...continued)

Premium."

[8] The 2013 Part B premium rates were published on November 21, 2012, *77 Federal Register 69850*, http://www.gpo.gov/fdsys/pkg/FR-2012-11-21/pdf/2012-28275.pdf.

[9] For additional information on Part A premiums, see **Appendix D**.

[10] For additional information on enrolling in Medicare, see Medicare publication "Understanding Medicare Enrollment Periods" at http://www.medicare.gov/Publications/Pubs/pdf/11219.pdf.

[11] See "Welcome to Medicare" publication at http://www.medicare.gov/Publications/Pubs/pdf/11095.pdf. When first becoming eligible for Medicare, beneficiaries need to make a number of choices regarding the benefits they wish to sign up for and how they wish to receive them. For example, new enrollees need to decide whether they wish to remain in traditional Medicare (Parts A and B, the default option) or if they would like to receive their A and B benefits through a private Medicare Advantage Plan (Part C). Additionally, beneficiaries will need to decide whether they would like to sign up for an outpatient prescription drug plan (Part D). These options are described in the "Welcome to (continued...)

A are also automatically enrolled in Part B.[12] However, because beneficiaries must pay a premium for Part B coverage, they have the option of turning it down.[13] Disabled persons who have received cash payments for 24 months under the Social Security or RRB disability programs also automatically receive a Medicare card and are enrolled in Part B unless they specifically decline such coverage.[14] Those who choose to receive coverage through a Medicare Advantage plan (Part C) must enroll in Part B.

Persons who are not receiving Social Security or RRB benefits, for example because they are still working or have not yet reached their full retirement benefit eligibility age,[15] must file an application with the Social Security Administration or RRB for Medicare benefits.[16] There are two kinds of enrollment periods, one that occurs when individuals are initially eligible for Medicare, and the later an annual general enrollment period for those who missed signing up during their initial enrollment period. A beneficiary may drop Part B enrollment and re-enroll an unlimited number of times, however premium penalties may be incurred.

Initial Enrollment Periods

Those who are not automatically enrolled in Medicare may sign up during a certain period when they first become eligible. The *initial enrollment* period is seven months long and begins three months before the month in which the individual first turns 65. (See **Table 1**.) Beneficiaries who do not file an application for Medicare benefits during their initial enrollment period could be subject to the Part B delayed enrollment penalty (see "Late-Enrollment Premium Penalty and Exceptions" below). If an individual accepts the automatic enrollment in Medicare Part B, or enrolls in Medicare Part B during the first three months of the initial enrollment period, coverage will start with the month in which an individual is first eligible, e.g., the month of the individual's 65th birthday. Those who enroll during the last four months, will have their coverage start date delayed from one to three months after enrollment.[17] The initial enrollment period of those

---

(...continued)

Medicare" package. For free personalized health insurance counseling, beneficiaries may contact their local State Health Insurance Assistance Programs (SHIPs); contact information may be found at http://www.medicare.gov/ contacts/ and https://www.shiptalk.org/About/SHIProfileSearchForm.aspx.

[12] Those who live in Puerto Rico are not enrolled in Medicare Part B automatically. They need to sign up for it during the initial enrollment period or possibly be subject to a penalty. H.R. 670, introduced in the 113th Congress, would extend this automatic enrollment to residents of Puerto Rico and create a special enrollment period and reduce late enrollment penalties for those who did not sign up for Part B when first eligible.

[13] Should a beneficiary decline Part B coverage, a new Medicare card will be issued that indicates that the beneficiary has Part A coverage only.

[14] Individuals with Amyotrophic Lateral Sclerosis (ALS) are not subject to the 24 month waiting period and Medicare coverage begins the first day of the month during which disability benefits start. Additionally, the Medicare coverage period for persons diagnosed with end-stage renal disease (ESRD) generally begins in the third month after the month when dialysis begins.

[15] In the past, individuals were generally eligible to receive both full Social Security retirement benefits and Medicare coverage starting at age 65. However, the age to receive full retirement benefits has changed for some people, depending on the year they were born. For example, some people won't be eligible for full Social Security benefits until age 67. See http://www.ssa.gov/pubs/10530.html.

[16] To apply, individuals can call or visit their local Social Security office or call Social Security at 1-800-772-1213. Some people may also apply online if they meet certain rules, at http://www.ssa.gov/medicareonly/. For RRB retirees, application information may be found at http://www.rrb.gov/forms/opa/rb20/rb20.asp.

[17] An eligibility and enrollment date calculator may be found on the Medicare.gov website at http://www.medicare.gov/ MedicareEligibility/home.asp?version=default&browser=IE%7C8%7CWindows+7&language=English.

eligible for Medicare based on disability or permanent kidney failure is linked to the date the disability or treatment began.[18]

Table 1. Initial Enrollment Period

Month of Enrollment and Effective Dates

	3 months before the month one turns 65	**The month during which one turns 65**	**Up to 3 months after the month one turns 65**
Effective Dates	If one signs up during the first 3 months of one's initial enrollment period, Part B coverage starts the 1st day of one's birthday month.[a]	If one enrolls during one's birthday month, the start date will be the 1st day of the next month.	The start date will be delayed if one enrolls during the last 3 months of the initial enrollment period. • If one signs up in the month after the month one turns 65, coverage starts 2 months after enrollment. • If one signs up 2 or 3 months after the month one turns 65, coverage starts 3 months after enrollment.
Example for someone turning 65 during the month of June The 7 month initial enrollment period would run from March 1st through September 30th.	If one enrolls in March, April, or May, coverage begins June 1st.	If one enrolls in June, coverage begins July 1st.	• If one enrolls in July, coverage begins September 1st. • If one enrolls in August, coverage begins November 1st. • If one enrolls in September, coverage begins December 1st.

Source: SSA Publication No. 05-10043.

a. If one's birthday falls on the 1st of the month, then the enrollment period starts a month earlier and coverage may begin on the 1st day of the month prior to one's birthday month.

General Enrollment Period

An individual who does not sign up for Medicare during the initial enrollment period must wait until the next *general enrollment* period. In addition, persons who decline Part B coverage when first eligible, or terminate Part B coverage, must also wait until the next general enrollment period to enroll or re-enroll. The general enrollment period lasts for three months from January 1st to March 31st of each year, with coverage beginning on July 1st of that year. A delayed enrollment penalty may apply.[19]

---

[18] For additional information on eligibility for the disabled under 65, see CRS Report RS22195, *Social Security Disability Insurance (SSDI) and Medicare: The 24-Month Waiting Period for SSDI Beneficiaries Under Age 65*, by Scott Szymendera.

[19] The Part B general enrollment period is different from the Medicare Advantage and Part D annual enrollment period which runs from October 15 to December 7 each year, with coverage effective the following January.

Late-Enrollment Premium Penalty and Exceptions

Beneficiaries who enroll in Part B after their initial enrollment period and/or reenroll after a termination of coverage may be subject to a "delayed enrollment penalty." In 2011, about 1.3% of Part B enrollees (about 600,000) paid this penalty.[20] On average, their total premiums (standard premium plus penalty) were about 32% higher than what they would have been had they not been subject to the penalty.

The penalty provision was included in the original Medicare legislation enacted in 1965 to help prevent adverse selection by creating a strong incentive for all eligible beneficiaries to enroll in Part B.[21] Adverse selection occurs when only those persons who think they need the benefits actually enroll in the program. When this happens, per capita costs are driven up, and premiums go up, thereby causing more persons (presumably the healthier, and less costly ones) to drop out of the program.[22] With most eligible persons over 65 enrolled in Part B, the costs are spread over the majority of this population and per capita costs are less than would be the case if adverse selection had occurred.

Those who receive premium assistance through a Medicare Savings Program do not pay this penalty; it is paid on their behalf by Medicaid. Additionally, for those disabled persons under 65 subject to a premium penalty, once the individual reaches age 65, he or she qualifies for a new enrollment period and would no longer pay a penalty.

Calculation of Penalty

The delayed enrollment penalty is equal to a 10% premium surcharge for each full 12 months of delay in enrollment and/or reenrollment during which the beneficiary was eligible for Medicare.[23] The length of the period equals: (1) the number of months that elapse between the end of the initial enrollment period and the end of the enrollment period in which the individual actually enrolls; or (2) for a person who re-enrolls, the months that elapse between the termination of coverage and the close of the enrollment period in which the individual enrolls.

Generally, individuals who do not enroll in Part B within a year of the end of their initial enrollment period would be subject to the premium penalty. For example, if an individual's initial enrollment period ended in September 2010 and the individual subsequently enrolled during the 2011 general enrollment period (January 1st through March 31st), the delay would be less than 12 months and the individual would not be subject to a penalty. However, if that individual delayed enrolling until the 2013 general enrollment period, the premium penalty would be 20%.

---

[20] Figures provided to CRS by the Centers for Medicare & Medicaid Services, March 2012.

[21] Social Security Act §1839(b).

[22] Specifically, adverse selection occurs when beneficiaries, who generally have more information than insurers about their own health status and expected health care needs, make insurance purchasing decisions based on their expected use of the insurance benefit. Their decision to purchase insurance is based on a comparison of the value of the insurance coverage, given their expected use, and the cost of the insurance. Should only (or disproportionately) persons who are high health care users enroll in the program, per capita costs would increase, thereby making the health insurance purchase decision less attractive for healthier, and presumably less costly, beneficiaries who then, in turn, might drop out of the program. Subsequent iterations of this cycle would drive premium costs higher and higher for a smaller and smaller subset of ever sicker and costlier beneficiaries.

[23] Social Security Act §1839(b).

(Although the elapsed time covers a total of 30 months of delayed enrollment, the episode includes only two full 12-month periods.) An individual who waits more than 10 years to enroll in Part B would pay twice the standard premium amount.

The surcharge is calculated as a percentage of the monthly standard premium amount (e.g., in 2013, $104.90), and that amount is added to the beneficiary's premium each month.[24] For the example above, in which the individual is subject to a 20% premium penalty, the total premium in 2013 would be calculated as follows:

Premium Penalty = Standard Premium x Applicable Percentage

Standard premium + Premium Penalty = Penalty Adjusted Premium

Example of a 20% penalty in 2013: $104.90 + ($104.90 x 20%) = $125.88

For those subject to the high-income premium (see "Income-Related Premium"), the late enrollment surcharge applies only to the standard monthly premium amount and not to the higher income adjustment portion of their premiums. Using the example above, should the beneficiary have an income of between $85,000 and $107,000, the applicable income-related adjustment of $42.00 would be added onto the penalty adjusted premium of $125.88, for a total monthly premium of $167.88.[25]

There is no upper limit on the amount of the surcharge that may apply, and the penalty continues to apply for the entire time the individual is enrolled in Part B. Each year the surcharge is calculated using the standard premium amount for that particular year. Therefore, if premiums increase in a given year, the dollar value of the surcharge will increase as well.

Exemptions to Penalty

Under certain conditions, select beneficiaries may be exempt from the delayed enrollment penalty. Beneficiaries who are exempt include working individuals (and their spouses) with group coverage, some military retirees, some international volunteers, and those who based their non-enrollment decision on incorrect information provided by a federal representative. Individuals who are permitted to delay enrollment have their own *special enrollment periods* (SEP).

---

[24] A late premium calculator may be found on the Medicare.gov website at http://www.medicare.gov/ MedicareEligibility/home.asp?dest= NAV%7CHome%7CResources%7CSurchargeCalcQuestions%7CResourcesOverview&version=default&browser= IE%7C8%7CWindows+7&language=English.

[25] For additional information, see SSA Programs Operation Manual Section HI 01101.031, "How IRMAA is Calculated and How IRMAA Affects the Total Medicare Premium," at https://secure.ssa.gov/apps10/poms nsf/lnx/0601101031.

Current Workers

A working individual and/or the spouse of a working individual may be able to delay enrollment in Medicare Part B without being subject to the delayed enrollment penalty. Delayed enrollment is permitted when an individual 65 or over has group health insurance coverage based on the individual's or spouse's *current employment* (with an employer with 20 or more employees). About 1.7 million of the 2.8 million working aged population are enrolled in Part A only, with most of the rest enrolled in both Parts A and B.[26] Delayed enrollment is also permitted for certain disabled persons who have group health insurance coverage based on their own or a family member's *current employment* with a large group health plan. For the disabled, a large group health plan is defined as one which covers 100 or more employees.

Specifically, persons permitted to delay coverage without penalty are those persons whose Medicare benefits are determined under the Medicare secondary payer (MSP) program.[27] Under MSP, an employer (with 20 or more employees) is required to offer workers aged 65 and over (and workers' spouses aged 65 and over) the same group health insurance coverage that is made available to other employees. The worker has the option of accepting or rejecting the employer's coverage. If he or she accepts the coverage, the employer plan is primary (i.e., pays benefits first) for the worker and/or spouse over age 65, and Medicare becomes the secondary payer (i.e., fills in the gaps in the employer plan, up to the limits of Medicare's coverage). Similarly, a group health plan offered by an employer with 100 or more employees is the primary payer for its employees under 65 years of age, or their dependents, who are entitled to Medicare because of disability.[28]

Such individuals may sign up for Medicare Part B (or Part A) anytime that they (or their spouse) are still working, and they are covered by a group health plan through the employer or union based on that work. Additionally, those who qualify for Medicare based on age (i.e., over 65), may sign up during the 8-month period after employment or group health plan coverage ends, *whichever happens first*. Disabled individuals whose group plan is involuntarily terminated have six months to enroll without penalty.[29]

Individuals who fail to enroll during this special enrollment period are considered to have delayed enrollment and thus could become subject to the penalty. For example, even though an individual may have continued health coverage through the former employer after retirement or have

---

[26] *Medicare Working-Aged Beneficiary Counts, Through December 2012*, from CMS 100% Unloaded Enrollment Database.

[27] Social Security Act § 1837(i) and 42 CFR § 407.20. See Medicare Publication "Medicare and Other Health Benefits: Your Guide to Who Pays First," http://www.medicare.gov/publications/pubs/pdf/02179.pdf and CMS Medicare Secondary Payer & You web page at https://www.cms.gov/Medicare/Coordination-of-Benefits/MedicareSecondPayerandYou/index html?redirect=/MedicareSecondPayerandYou/.

[28] For Medicare-eligible beneficiaries employed by organizations with fewer than 20 employees (or fewer than 100 employees for the disabled), Medicare generally pays primary and the employer group health plan is secondary. In such cases, employers may offer coverage that wraps around the Medicare benefit, and beneficiaries would need to enroll in Medicare Part B when first eligible to avoid a gap in coverage. Individuals who are turning 65 and still working should check with their employers' benefit administrator to learn how their employer health coverage works with Medicare.

[29] The Balanced Budget Act of 1997 (BBA, P.L. 105-33) added this exception to the penalty. This exception is for disabled persons who: (a) at the time they first become eligible for Part B are enrolled in a group health plan (regardless of size) by virtue of their current or former employment, and (b) whose continuous enrollment under the plan is involuntarily terminated at a time when their enrollment in the plan is by virtue of their or their spouse's former (i.e., not current) employment. These individuals have a special six-month enrollment period beginning on the first day of the month in which the termination occurs.

COBRA coverage, he or she must sign up for Part B within 8 months of retiring to avoid paying a Part B penalty if the individual eventually enrolls. Individuals who return to work and receive health care coverage through that employment may be able to drop Part B coverage, qualify for a new special enrollment period upon leaving that employment, and re-enroll in Part B again without penalty as long as enrollment is completed within the specified timeframe.

Certain Military Retirees

Some military retirees may also be exempt from the late enrollment penalty. Health care coverage for military retirees was expanded by the Floyd D. Spence National Defense Authorization Act for FY2001 (P.L. 106-398). This law established the TRICARE For Life (TFL) program, which acts as a secondary payer to Medicare and provides supplemental coverage to TRICARE-eligible beneficiaries who are entitled to Medicare Part A and have Medicare Part B, based on age, disability, or end-stage renal disease (ESRD). The Patient Protection and Affordable Care Act (ACA, P.L. 111-148, Section 3110) establishes a 12-month special enrollment period (SEP) for certain individuals who are otherwise eligible for TRICARE and are entitled to Medicare Part A based on disability or ESRD, but have declined Part B. The Secretary of Defense is required to identify and notify individuals of their eligibility for this Special Enrollment Period. The SEP begins the first day of the month following the end of the individual's initial enrollment period, or if later, the month the individual is notified that s/he is entitled to Medicare Part A and Part B. The late enrollment surcharge is waived for those who enroll during the SEP. (If the individual does not enroll during the SEP, he or she may only enroll during the General Enrollment Period and the late enrollment surcharge could apply.)

International Volunteers

Some international volunteers may also be exempt from the Part B late enrollment penalty. The Deficit Reduction Act of 2005 (P.L. 109-171) permits certain individuals to delay enrollment in Part B without a delayed enrollment penalty if they volunteered outside of the United States for at least 12 months through a program sponsored by a tax-exempt organization defined under Section 501(c)(3) of the Internal Revenue Code.[30] The individuals must demonstrate they had health insurance coverage while serving in the international program. Individuals permitted to delay enrollment have a six-month special enrollment period, which begins on the first day of the first month they no longer qualify under this provision.

Equitable Relief

Under certain circumstances, a special enrollment period may be created and/or late enrollment penalties may be waived if a Medicare beneficiary can establish that an error, misrepresentation, or inaction of a federal worker or an agent of the federal government (such as an employee of the Social Security Administration (SSA), CMS, or a Medicare administrative contractor) resulted in late Part B enrollment.[31] In order to qualify for an exception under these conditions, the beneficiary must provide documentary evidence of the error, which "can be in the form of

---

[30] Social Security Act §1837(k) and 42 CFR §407.21.

[31] Social Security Act §1837(h) and 42 CFR §407.32.

statements from employees, agents, or persons in authority that the alleged misinformation, misadvice, misrepresentation, inaction, or erroneous action actually occurred."[32]

Collection of the Part B Premium

If a person is enrolled in both Medicare Part B and Social Security, the Part B premiums are deducted from the person's Social Security benefit.[33] In addition, railroad retirees and civil service annuitants have their Part B premiums deducted from their monthly checks when possible. This withholding does not apply to those beneficiaries receiving state public assistance through a Medicare Savings Program as their premiums are paid by their state Medicaid program (see "Premium Assistance for Low-Income Beneficiaries"). Beneficiaries who are not entitled to a monthly cash benefit from Social Security, a railroad retirement annuity or pension, or a federal civil service annuity must pay the Part B premium directly to CMS.[34]

Deduction of Part B Premiums from Social Security Checks

Ultimately, everyone who is eligible for Social Security retirement or disability benefits qualifies for Medicare. Most people who elect to participate in the Part B program pay the Medicare Part B premium.[35] By law, a Social Security beneficiary who is also enrolled in Medicare Part B must have the Part B premium automatically deducted from his or her Social Security benefits.[36] Automatic deduction from the Social Security benefit check also applies to Medicare Advantage participants, who are enrolled in private health-care plans in lieu of traditional Medicare.[37]

About 65% of Social Security beneficiaries (37 million persons) have Medicare Part B premiums deducted from their benefit checks.[38] Social Security beneficiaries who do not pay Medicare Part B premiums include those who are under the age of 65 and don't yet qualify for Medicare (e.g., began receiving Social Security benefits at age 62), receive low-income assistance from Medicaid to pay the Part B premium, have started to receive Social Security disability insurance (SSDI) but are not eligible for Medicare Part B because they have not received SSDI for 24 months, or chose not to enroll in Medicare Part B.

---

[32] For additional information, see Social Security Program Operations Manual Section HI 00805.170 *Conditions for Providing Equitable Relief*, https://secure.ssa.gov/poms nsf/lnx/0600805170 and Section HI 00805.175 *Evidence of Government Error or Delay*, https://secure.ssa.gov/poms nsf/lnx/0600805175.

[33] Social Security Act §1840(a)(1).

[34] 42 C.F.R. §408.60.

[35] Some beneficiaries do not pay Medicare premiums because they receive low-income assistance.

[36] Social Security Act §1840(a)(1).

[37] Beneficiaries who receive their Parts A and B benefits through Medicare Advantage (MA, Part C), must still pay the monthly Part B premium, but may pay different amounts. For example, some MA plans may offer an additional benefit by reducing the amount one pays for the Part B premium. Alternatively, some MA plans may be more expensive than traditional Medicare, for example because they provide benefits beyond what is provided under traditional Medicare, and may charge an additional premium in addition to the Part B premium. SSA has in place a "safety net" to prevent the deduction of more than $300 of Part C and Part D plan premiums from a single Social Security check. For amounts over $300, the enrollee may be billed directly.

[38] Number of people as of January 2013. Figures provided to CRS by the Social Security Administration.

The amount of an individual's Social Security benefits cannot go down one year to the next as a result of the annual Part B premium increase, except in the case of higher-income individuals subject to income-related premiums. (See "Protection of Social Security Benefits from Increases in Medicare Part B Premiums.") For those beneficiaries "held-harmless," the dollar amount of their Part B premium increases would be held below or equal to the amount of the increase in their monthly Social Security benefits.

Part B Enrollees Who Do Not Receive Social Security Benefits

About 2% of Medicare Part B enrollees do not receive Social Security benefits. For example, certain persons who spent their careers in employment that was not covered by Social Security, including certain federal, state, or local government workers, and certain other categories of workers, do not receive Social Security benefits, but may still qualify for Medicare. For those who receive benefit payments from the Railroad Retirement Board (RRB),[39] or the Civil Service Civil Service Retirement System,[40] Part B premiums are deducted from the enrollees' monthly benefit payments but net retirement benefit amounts are not "held harmless" from increases in the Part B premium. For those who do not receive these types of benefit payments, Medicare will bill directly for their premiums every 3 months.[41] Nonpayment of premiums results in termination of enrollment in the Part B program, although a grace period (through the last day of the third month following the month of the due date) is allowed for beneficiaries who are billed and pay directly.[42]

Determining the Part B Premium

Each year, the CMS actuaries estimate total per capita Part B costs for beneficiaries aged 65 and older over for the following year and set the Part B premium to cover 25% of these expected expenditures.[43] However, because prospective estimates may differ from the actual spending for the year, contingency reserve adjustments are made to ensure sufficient income to accommodate potential variation in actual expenditures during the year. The Part B premium is a single national amount that does not vary with a beneficiary's age, health status or place of residence. Premiums may be adjusted, however, for late enrollment (see "Late-Enrollment Premium Penalty and Exceptions") and for beneficiaries with high incomes (see "Income-Related Premiums").

---

[39] Social Security Act §1840(b)(1).

[40] Generally, employees of the federal government hired before 1984 are covered by the Civil Service Retirement System (CSRS) and are not covered by Social Security. Most federal workers first hired into federal service on or after January 1984, participate in the Federal Employees' Retirement System (FERS) which includes Social Security coverage.

[41] Payment may be made by check, money order, or credit card; or one may schedule it to be automatically deducted from one's bank account. Premium billing form and information may be found at https://secure.ssa.gov/poms nsf/lnx/0600825914.

[42] This grace period may be extended for up to an additional three months if the enrollee can establish that non-payment was due to circumstances beyond his or her control, such as being physically or mentally incapable of making premium payments or due to an administrative error.

[43] Part B premium announcements are generally made in the fall prior to the effective year. For example, the Part B premium rate was announced in November of 2012.

Premium Calculation for 2013[44]

Monthly Part B premiums are based on the estimated amount that would be needed to finance Part B expenditures on an incurred basis during the year. In estimating needed income and to account for potential variation, CMS takes into consideration the difference in prior years of estimated and actual program costs, the likelihood and potential impact of potential legislation affecting Part B in the coming year, and the expected relationship between incurred and cash expenditures (e.g., payments for some services provided during a particular year may not be paid until the following year). Once the premium has been set for a year, it will not be changed during that year.

While both aged and disabled Medicare beneficiaries may enroll in Part B, the statute provides that Part B premiums are to be based only on the expected benefit costs, i.e., the *monthly actuarial rate*, for the aged (those over 65). (See **Appendix A** for a discussion of the history of the premium methodology.) Part B costs not covered by premiums are paid for through transfers from the general fund of the Treasury. The monthly actuarial rates for *both* the aged and disabled enrollees are used to determine the needed amount of general revenue funding per beneficiary each month (one-half of the expected average monthly cost for each aged enrollee and one-half of the expected cost for each disabled enrollee).

To determine the 2013 monthly Part B premium amount, CMS first estimated the monthly actuarial rate for enrollees age 65 and older using actual per-enrollee costs by type of service from program data through 2011 and projected these costs for subsequent years. For 2013, CMS estimated that the monthly amount needed to cover one-half of the total benefit and administration costs for the aged would be $198.11. However, because of expected variations between projected and actual costs, a contingency adjustment of $14.07 was added to this amount (see "Contingency Reserve" below). After a reduction of $2.38 to account for expected interest on trust fund assets, the monthly actuarial rate for the aged was determined to be $209.80. As premiums are only based on projections of expected costs of the aged, and the actuarial monthly amount for the aged accounts for one-half of projections of total costs (with the actuarial monthly amount for the disabled making up the other half), the 2013 Part B premium amount is one-half of $209.80, or $104.90 per month (25% of the monthly expected per capita costs of the aged).

Contingency Reserve

The contingency reserve is the amount set aside to cover an appropriate degree of variation between actual and projected costs. In recent years, CMS has noted that Part B expenditures have been higher than expected under current law.[45] In some cases, legislation that resulted in increased Medicare Part B expenditures for the year was enacted after the premium for the year had been set. For example, current law specifies a physician payment formula called the sustainable growth rate system (SGR) for calculating the annual update to the conversion factor

---

[44] "Medicare Program: Medicare Part B Monthly Actuarial Rates, Premium Rate, and Annual Deductible Beginning January 1, 2013," 77 *Federal Register* 69850, November 21, 2012,http://www.gpo.gov/fdsys/pkg/FR-2012-11-21/pdf/2012-28275.pdf.

[45] Centers for Medicare & Medicaid Services, "Medicare Program: Medicare Part B Monthly Actuarial Rates, Premium Rate, and Annual Deductible Beginning January 1, 2013," 77 *Federal Register* 69850, November 21, 2012, http://www.gpo.gov/fdsys/pkg/FR-2012-11-21/pdf/2012-28275.pdf.

---

used to determine payments under the physician fee schedule.[46] The SGR formula has called for a reduction in the update factor (i.e., lower reimbursement rates) for each year since 2003. However, Congress has overridden the payment cut in every year except one, by passing legislation that has either frozen or slightly increased the reimbursement rates. These actions have often led to discrepancies between the actual and projected Part B costs.

In calculating the premium for 2013, CMS recognized the possibility that Congress would override the scheduled reduction of about 27% in physician fees for 2013 (thereby significantly increasing Part B expenses), and provided for the maintenance of a somewhat higher contingency reserve than would otherwise be necessary in calculating the 2013 premium.[47]

Additionally, CMS assumed that the reduction in Medicare benefit payments under the Budget Control Act of 2011 (P.L. 112-25) scheduled to start in 2013 would be modified or postponed.[48] CMS estimated that Part B expenditures would be reduced by $4.3 billion in 2013 under sequestration. The contingency margin was adjusted to accommodate the possibility that sequestration would not occur.[49]

Additionally, starting in 2011, manufacturers and importers of brand-name drugs began paying a fee that is allocated to the SMI trust fund. The contingency reserve was thus reduced to account for this additional revenue. Further, certain payment incentives to encourage the development and use of health information technology (HIT) by Medicare physicians, are excluded from premium determinations. (HIT bonuses or penalties will be directly offset through transfers of general funds from the Treasury.) The downward 2013 contingency margin adjustment of $14.07 reflects the expected net effects of all of these factors.

Income-Related Premiums

For the first forty-one years of the Medicare program, all Part B enrollees paid the same Part B premium regardless of their income. However, the Medicare Modernization Act of 2003 (MMA; P.L. 108-173)[50] required that, beginning in 2007, high-income enrollees pay higher premiums.[51] About 4% of Part B enrollees were estimated to have paid this higher premium in 2012.[52]

---

[46] For additional information on the Medicare physician rate system, see CRS Report R40907, *Medicare Physician Payment Updates and the Sustainable Growth Rate (SGR) System*, by Jim Hahn and Janemarie Mulvey.

[47] The American Taxpayer Relief Act of 2012 (P.L. 112-240), signed into law on January 2, 2013, prevented the reduction in Medicare physician payment rates slated to begin on January 1, 2013, and instead froze payment rates at their current level though December 31, 2013.

[48] For a comprehensive discussion of the BCA, see CRS Report R41965, *The Budget Control Act of 2011*, by Bill Heniff Jr., Elizabeth Rybicki, and Shannon M. Mahan. For Medicare specific rules under BCA, see CRS Report R42050, *Budget "Sequestration" and Selected Program Exemptions and Special Rules*, coordinated by Karen Spar.

[49] The American Taxpayer Relief Act of 2012 (P.L. 112-240), signed into law on January 2, 2013, postponed the automatic reduction by two months. See CRS Report R42884, *The "Fiscal Cliff" and the American Taxpayer Relief Act of 2012*, coordinated by Mindy R. Levit. No additional action has been taken, and payment reductions are scheduled to go into effect in April 2013.

[50] The MMA would have phased in the increase over five years; however, the Deficit Reduction Act of 2005 (DRA, P.L. 109-171) shortened the phase-in period to three years.

[51] At the time of enactment of the MMA, the Congressional Budget Office (CBO) estimated that 1.2 million persons (3% of beneficiaries) would pay higher premiums in 2007; and 2.8 million persons (6% of beneficiaries) would pay higher premiums in 2013. CBO further estimated that the MMA provision would reduce federal outlays by $13.3 (continued...)

Adjustments are made to the Part B premiums for high-income beneficiaries with the share of expenditures paid by beneficiaries increasing with income. This share ranges from 35% to 80% of the value of Part B coverage. In 2013, individuals whose income exceeds $85,000, and couples whose income exceeds $170,000, are subject to higher premium amounts. Income thresholds used in determining high-income Part B premiums for 2011 through 2019 are frozen at the 2010 levels.[53] The current law provision that prevents a beneficiary's Social Security benefits from decreasing from one year to the next as a result of the Part B premium increase does not apply to those subject to an income-related increase in their Part B premiums. (See "Protection of Social Security Benefits from Increases in Medicare Part B Premiums.")

Determination of Income

To determine those subject to the high-income premium, Social Security uses the most recent Federal tax return provided by IRS. In general, the taxable year used in determining the premium is the second calendar year preceding the applicable year. For example, the 2012 tax return (2011 income) was used to determine who would pay the 2013 high-income premiums.[54]

High-income adjustments to Part B premiums are referred to as the *income-related monthly adjustment amount* (IRMAA). The income definition on which these premiums are based is modified adjusted gross income (MAGI) which is different from total income. Specifically, gross income equals total income (from all sources) minus certain exclusions (e.g., nontaxable Social Security benefits). From gross income, adjusted gross income (AGI) is calculated to reflect a number of deductions, including trade and business deductions, losses from sale of property, and alimony payments. MAGI is defined as AGI[55] plus certain foreign earned income and tax-exempt interest.[56]

If a person had a one-time increase in taxable income in a particular year (such as from the sale of income producing property), that increase would be considered in determining the individual's total income for that year and thus liability for the income-related premium two years ahead. It would not be considered in the calculations for future years.

(...continued)

billion over the 2007-2013 period. CBO estimated that the DRA provision accelerating the phase-in would increase premium collections by $1.6 billion over the 2007-2010 period. The MMA estimate and the DRA estimate were each made by CBO at the time of enactment of each law. Both estimates were based on the CBO budget baseline in effect at the time. As is the case for all CBO estimates, the earlier estimates are incorporated into subsequent CBO baselines. Therefore the two savings estimates cannot be added together.

[52] Centers for Medicare & Medicaid Services, "Medicare Program: Medicare Part B Monthly Actuarial Rates, Premium Rate, and Annual Deductible Beginning January 1, 2013," 77 *Federal Register* 69850, November 21, 2012, http://www.gpo.gov/fdsys/pkg/FR-2012-11-21/pdf/2012-28275.pdf.

[53] Section 3402 of the Patient Protection and Affordable Care Act (P.L. 111-148).

[54] If an enrollee amended his or her tax return and it changed the income used to determine the high-income adjustments, the updated information should be provided to Social Security so that it may correct or remove the income-related monthly adjustment amounts.

[55] Internal Revenue Code, Section 62.

[56] The definition of MAGI for IRMAA in Medicare is different from the MAGI definition in certain ACA Medicaid provisions. See CRS Report R41997, *Definition of Income for Certain Medicaid Provisions and Premium Credits in ACA*, coordinated by Janemarie Mulvey.

In the case of certain major life-changing events that result in a significant reduction in modified MAGI, an individual may request to have the determination made for a more recent year than the second preceding year.[57] Major life-changing events include (1) death of a spouse; (2) marriage; (3) divorce or annulment; (4) partial or full work stoppage for the individual or spouse; (5) loss by individual or spouse of income from income-producing property when the loss is not at the individual's direction (such as in the case of a natural disaster); or (6) reduction or loss for individual or spouse of pension income due to termination or reorganization of the plan or scheduled cessation of the pension.

If Medicare enrollees disagree with decisions regarding their income-related monthly adjustment amounts, they may file an appeal with Social Security. Enrollees may either submit a "Request for Reconsideration"[58] or contact their local Social Security office to file an appeal. (An enrollee does not need to file an appeal if he or she is requesting a new decision based on a life-changing event described above, or if the enrollee has shown that Social Security used the wrong information to make the original decision.)

Income Thresholds and Premium Adjustments

Depending on their level of income, beneficiaries may be classified into one of five income categories.[59] In 2013, individuals with incomes less than $85,000 a year ($170,000 for a couple) pay the standard premium which is based on 25% of the average Part B per capita cost. Individuals with income over $85,000 per year and couples with income over $170,000 per year pay a higher percentage of Part B costs. Depending on one's level of income over these threshold amounts, premiums may be adjusted to cover 35%, 50%, 65%, or 80% of the value of Part B coverage (with the rest being subsidized through federal general revenues). The five income categories and associated premiums for 2013 are shown below in **Table 2**. When both members of a couple are enrolled in Part B, each pays the applicable premium amount.

---

[57] Social Security Form SSA-44, http://www.ssa.gov/online/ssa-44.pdf.

[58] Social Security Form SSA-561-U2, http://www.ssa.gov/online/ssa-561.pdf.

[59] Social Security Act §1839(i).

Table 2. Monthly Medicare Part B Premiums for 2013

Levels of Premium Adjustment and Percentage of Costs Covered by Premiums	Beneficiaries who file an individual tax return with income:	Beneficiaries who file a joint tax return with income:	Income-Related Monthly Adjustment Amount (IRMAA)	Total Monthly Premium (standard premium + adjustment)
Standard = 25%	Less than or equal to $85,000	Less than or equal to $170,000	$0.00	$104.90
Level 1 = 35%	Greater than $85,000 and less than or equal to $107,000	Greater than $170,000 and less than or equal to $214,000	$42.00	$146.90
Level 2 = 50%	Greater than $107,000 and less than or equal to $160,000	Greater than $214,000 and less than or equal to $320,000	$104.90	$209.80
Level 3 = 65%	Greater than $160,000 and less than or equal to $214,000	Greater than $320,000 and less than or equal to $428,000	$167.80	$272.70
Level 4 = 80%	Greater than $214,000	Greater than $428,000	$230.80	$335.70

Source: Centers for Medicare & Medicaid Services, "Medicare Program: Medicare Part B Monthly Actuarial Rates, Premium Rate, and Annual Deductible Beginning January 1, 2013," 77 *Federal Register* 69850, November 21, 2012, http://www.gpo.gov/fdsys/pkg/FR-2012-11-21/pdf/2012-28275.pdf.

Married persons who lived with their spouse at some point during the year, but who filed separate returns, are subject to different premium amounts. There are two higher income categories that determine the additional monthly premium adjustment for these beneficiaries. The income levels and premium amounts are shown in **Table 3**.

Table 3. Part B Premium Adjustment for Married Beneficiaries Filing Separately for 2013

Beneficiaries who are married and lived with their spouse at any time during the year, but file a separate tax return from their spouse:	Income-Related Monthly Adjustment Amount (IRMAA)	Total Monthly Premium (standard premium +adjustment)
Less than or equal to $85,000	$0.00	$104.90
Greater than $85,000 and less than or equal to $129,000	$167.80	$272.70
Greater than $129,000	$230.80	$335.70

Source: "Medicare Program: Medicare Part B Monthly Actuarial Rates, Premium Rate, and Annual Deductible Beginning January 1, 2013," 77 *Federal Register* 69850, November 21, 2012, http://www.gpo.gov/fdsys/pkg/FR-2012-11-21/pdf/2012-28275.pdf.

The original provision establishing the Part B income related premiums set the initial income threshold and high-income level ranges. Prior to 2010, annual adjustments to these levels were based on annual changes in the consumer price index for urban consumers (CPI-U), rounded to the nearest $1,000. However, the ACA froze the income thresholds and ranges at the 2010 level through 2019, rather than allowing them to rise with inflation.[60] Therefore, the thresholds will

---

[60] Section 3402 of the ACA (P.L. 111-148). Because more beneficiaries are expected to pay this higher premium over time and therefore reduce the amount of general revenues needed to fund Part B, CBO scored this provision as saving the federal government $25 billion over 10 years (FY2010-FY2019), http://www.cbo.gov/sites/default/files/cbofiles/ (continued...)

remain at $85,000 and $170,000 through 2019. This means that over time, as income rises with inflation, including increases in Social Security benefits, a greater share of Medicare enrollees may pay the high-income premiums. In 2020 and subsequent years, the income thresholds are again to be indexed to inflation as if they had not been frozen between 2011 and 2019.

Premium Assistance for Low-Income Beneficiaries

Medicare beneficiaries with limited income and resources may be able to qualify for assistance with their premiums and other out-of-pocket expenses.[61] About one in five Medicare beneficiaries receives Part B premium subsidies.

Medicare beneficiaries who qualify for full Medicaid benefits (full dual-eligibles) have the majority of their health care expenses paid for by either Medicare or Medicaid. For these individuals, Medicaid covers the majority of Medicare premium and cost-sharing expenses, and supplements Medicare by providing coverage for services not covered under Medicare, such as dental services and long-term services and supports (LTSS). In cases where services are covered by both Medicare and Medicaid, Medicare pays first and Medicaid picks up most of the remaining costs. Each state has different rules about eligibility and applying for Medicaid.[62]

Beneficiaries who do not meet their respective state's eligibility criteria for Medicaid may still qualify for assistance with Part B premiums if they have incomes of less than 135% of the federal poverty level (FPL) and assets of less than $7,080 for an individual or $10,620 for a couple in 2013.[63] These assistance programs are commonly referred to as *Medicare Savings Programs* (MSP).[64] Eligible individuals fall into one of the following coverage groups:

Qualified Medicare Beneficiaries (QMBs)

Aged or disabled persons with incomes at or below FPL may qualify for the QMB program.[65] In 2013, the QMB monthly qualifying income levels are $958 for individuals and $1,293 for a

---

(...continued)

ftpdocs/113xx/doc11379/amendreconprop.pdf.

[61] See Medicare.gov, "Help with Medical and Drug Costs" at http://www.medicare.gov/navigation/medicare-basics/ medical-and-drug-costs.aspx. Subsidies are also available for low-income beneficiaries enrolled in Part D, the outpatient prescription drug benefit. Those who are eligible for assistance with Part B premiums through their Medicaid programs are automatically eligible to receive the Part D low-income subsidy. Other low-income beneficiaries with incomes below 150% of the federal poverty level, and who meet the resource tests, may also be eligible for the drug subsidy.

[62] See CRS Report RL33202, *Medicaid: A Primer*, by Elicia J. Herz.

[63] Income and asset requirements may vary by state and change each year. These amounts do not include a burial fund allowance of $1,500 per person.

[64] For additional information about these programs and to learn whether a beneficiary might qualify for Medicare premium assistance, one should contact one's State Medical Assistance (Medicaid) office. (As the names of these programs may vary by state, one should specifically inquire about Medicare Savings Programs.) The contact information for state Medicaid offices may be obtained by calling 1-800-MEDICARE (1-800-633-4227) or by visiting the following Medicare website: http://www.medicare.gov/contacts.

[65] The federal poverty levels for 2013 are $11,490 per year for an individual and $15,510 for a couple. (These levels are slightly higher in Alaska and Hawaii.) See *The 2013 HHS Poverty Guidelines* at http://aspe.hhs.gov/poverty/ 13poverty.cfm.

---

couple (annual income of $11,490 and $15,510, respectively).[66] QMBs are entitled to have their Medicare Parts A and B cost-sharing charges, including the Part B premium and all deductibles and coinsurance, paid for by Medicaid.[67] (See **Table 4**.) For QMBs, Medicaid coverage is limited to the payment of Medicare cost-sharing charges (i.e., the Medicare beneficiary is *not* entitled to coverage of Medicaid plan services, unless the individual is otherwise entitled to Medicaid).

Table 4. 2013 Medicare Savings Program Eligibility Standards

	Monthly Income[a]	Resources[b]	Benefits
Qualified Medicare Beneficiary (QMB)	**At or below 100% FPL[c]** $958 – single $1,293 – couple	$7,080 – single $10,620 – couple	Part B premium[d] Coverage of Parts A and B deductibles and coinsurance
Specified Low-Income Medicare Beneficiary (SLMB)	**Above 100% but less than 120% FPL[c]** $958.01 – $1,149 – single $1,293.01 – $1,551 – couple	$7,080 – single $10,620 – couple	Part B premium
Qualifying Individual (QI)	**At or above 120% but less than 135% FPL[c]** $1,149.01 – $1,293 – single $1,551.01 – $1,745 – couple	$7,080 – single $10,620 – couple	Part B premium

Source: Social Security Program Operations Manual Section HI 00815.023 (Income Limits), https://secure.ssa.gov/poms.nsf/lnx/0600815023, and CRS calculations based on the 2013 FPL Poverty Guidelines, http://aspe.hhs.gov/poverty/13poverty.cfm.

a. These amounts do not include a $20 general income exclusion where $20 from any income is not counted towards these income limits; in most cases, $20 may be added to the above monthly income limits.

b. Resources include money in checking and savings accounts, stocks, bonds, mutual funds, and Individual Retirement Accounts (IRAs). Resources don't include one's primary residence, a life insurance policy worth up to $1,500, one car, burial plots, up to $1,500 per person for burial expenses, and household items. Some states have no limits on resources.

c. Federal Poverty Levels (FPLs) are updated each year, usually in January or February. Income levels are higher for Hawaii and Alaska and for those living with dependents.

d. Most people do not pay a premium for Part A because they have worked 40 or more quarters in covered employment. For those without sufficient work history to qualify for premium-free Part A, Medicaid will also pay Part A premiums for QMBs.

Specified Low-Income Medicare Beneficiaries (SLMBs)

Individuals whose income is more than 100% but less than 120% of FPL may qualify for assistance as a SLMB. In 2013, the monthly income limits are $1,149 for an individual and

---

[66] The qualifying levels are slightly higher than the monthly federal poverty level because, by law, $20 per month of unearned income is disregarded in the calculation. See SSA Program Operations Manual HI 00815.023 Medicare Savings Programs Income Limits at https://secure.ssa.gov/poms.nsf/lnx/0600815023.

[67] The QMB program does not provide assistance with drug costs. Low-income beneficiaries who qualify for a Medicare Savings Program are automatically enrolled in Medicare Part D; their premiums and most cost-sharing is paid for by the Part D low-income subsidy which is financed through Medicare. States pay some of the costs for Part D low-income assistance through state transfer payments.

$1,551 for a couple (annual income of $13,788 and $18,612, respectively).[68] Medicaid pays the Medicare Part B premiums for SLMBs, but not other cost-sharing.

Qualifying Individuals (QIs)

Individuals whose income is between 120% and 135% of the federal poverty level may qualify for assistance as QIs. In 2013, the monthly income limit for a QI is $1,293, and for a couple, $1,745 (annual income of $15,512 and $20,939, respectively). Medicaid protection for these individuals is limited to payment of the monthly Medicare Part B premium. Expenditures under the QI program are, however, paid for (100%) by the federal government from the Medicare SMI trust fund up to the state's allocation level.[69] A state is only required to cover the number of people who would bring its spending on these population groups in a year up to its allocation level. Any expenditures beyond that level are voluntary and paid entirely by the state.

Funding for the QI program was first made available by the Balanced Budget Act of 1997 (BBA97; P.L. 105-33),[70] and was continued through subsequent legislation. Most recently, the American Taxpayer Relief Act of 2012 (P.L. 112-240) extended the program and the amounts available through allocation until December 31, 2013.[71]

Protection of Social Security Benefits from Increases in Medicare Part B Premiums

After a person becomes eligible to receive Social Security benefits, his or her monthly benefit amount is increased annually to maintain purchasing power over time. Near the end of each year, the Social Security Administration announces the cost-of-living adjustment (COLA) payable in January of the following year. The amount of the COLA is based on inflation as measured by the Consumer Price Index-Urban Wage Earners and Clerical Workers (CPI-W).[72] If the CPI-W decreases, Social Security benefits stay the same—benefits are not reduced during periods of deflation.

In instances when the annual Social Security COLA is not sufficient to cover the standard Medicare Part B premium increase, most beneficiaries are protected by a *hold harmless* provision in the Social Security Act.[73] Specifically, if in a given year, the increase in the standard Part B premium would cause a beneficiary's Social Security check to be less, in dollar terms, than it was the year before, then the Part B premium is reduced to ensure that the amount of the individual's

---

[68] The qualifying levels are calculated the same way as for the QMB program.

[69] In general, Medicaid payments are normally shared between the federal government and the states according to matching formulas.

[70] Section 4732(c) of BBA97 added §1933(c) of the Social Security Act.

[71] See CRS Report R42944, *Medicare, Medicaid, and Other Health Provisions in the American Taxpayer Relief Act of 2012*, coordinated by Jim Hahn.

[72] The CPI-W tracks the prices of a fixed market basket of goods and services over time. Social Security's COLA is calculated as the change in the CPI-W from the third quarter of the prior calendar year to the third quarter of the current calendar year. If the CPI-W increases during this period, Social Security benefits for the next year increase proportionately. See CRS Report 94-803, *Social Security: Cost-of-Living Adjustments*, by Gary Sidor.

[73] Social Security Act §1839(f). The hold harmless provision was first implemented in January 1987.

Social Security check does not decline.[74] To be held harmless in a given year, a Social Security beneficiary must have received Social Security benefit checks in both December of the previous year and January of the current year, and must also have had Part B premiums deducted from both checks.[75] The hold harmless provision operates by comparing the net dollar amounts of the two monthly benefit payments—if the net Social Security benefit for January of the current year is lower than in December of the previous year, then the hold harmless provision takes effect for most individuals.[76] This determination is made by the Social Security Administration.

Several groups are *not* covered by the hold harmless provision.

- **Lower-Income Beneficiaries.** Lower-income beneficiaries who receive premium subsidies are not held harmless for premium increases; however, the Medicaid program pays the full amount of any increase in their Part B premiums. (See "Premium Assistance for Low-Income Beneficiaries.")

- **Higher-Income Beneficiaries.** Higher-income beneficiaries who are required to pay income-related Part B premiums are not held harmless for premium increases. They are required to pay the full amount of any increase in their Part B premiums. (See "Income-Related Premiums.")

- **Beneficiaries with no history of Social Security benefit checks with deductions to cover the Medicare Part B premium.** This includes new enrollees in either Social Security or Medicare Part B, and Part B enrollees who do not receive Social Security benefits. As noted above, in order to be held harmless in a given year, a Social Security beneficiary must have received Social Security benefit payments in both December of the previous year and January of the current year, and must have had Part B premiums deducted from both checks. (See "Part B Enrollees Who Do Not Receive Social Security Benefits.")

As described earlier, an individual's Social Security COLA is determined by multiplying his or her benefit amount by the inflation rate (i.e., the CPI-W). Part B premiums are determined by projected Part B program costs. Thus, the number of people held harmless can vary widely from year to year, depending on annual inflation rates and projected Part B costs. For most years, the hold harmless provision has affected a relatively small number of beneficiaries. However, due to low inflation, no COLA adjustments were made to Social Security benefits in 2010 and 2011. Most Medicare beneficiaries (about 73%) were protected by the hold harmless provision and continued to pay the 2009 standard monthly premium of $96.40 in both 2010 and 2011.[77] Because

---

[74] For more information on the hold harmless provision, see CRS Report R40561, *Interactions Between the Social Security COLA and Medicare Part B Premiums*, by Jim Hahn.

[75] Note that Social Security benefit checks reflect benefit entitlements for the previous month while Part B premiums are deducted in advance. For example, a November Social Security benefit check is not received until December, but has December's Part B premium deducted from it.

[76] Part D premiums are not covered by the hold harmless provision; therefore some people protected by the Part B hold harmless provision may still see a decrease in their Social Security checks due to an increase in Medicare Part D premiums. Beneficiaries who qualify for the Part D low-income subsidies, however, would not be affected.

[77] The standard Part B premium in 2009 was also the same as that in 2008, $96.40; however, the lack of change in those years was not a result of the "hold harmless" provision. At the end of 2008, it was determined that Part B premiums and general revenue financing in recent years had been set at somewhat higher levels than would otherwise be required to maintain an adequate contingency reserve, and that the level of assets in the Part B account of the SMI trust fund were more than adequate. Therefore, it was estimated that an adequate level of assets could be maintained throughout the next year, 2009, without an increase in premiums.

Part B expenditures were still expected to increase in those years, and beneficiary premiums are required to cover 25% of those costs, the premiums for those not held harmless (27% of beneficiaries) were higher than they would have been had the rest of the beneficiaries not been held harmless. The standard monthly premiums paid by those not held harmless was $110.50 in 2010 and $115.40 in 2011.[78] In 2011, of the 27% who were not eligible to be held harmless, about 3% were new enrollees, about 5% were high-income, about 17% had their premiums paid for by Medicaid, and the remaining 2% did not have their premiums withheld from Social Security benefit payments.

In 2012, Social Security beneficiaries received a 3.6% COLA which increased the average monthly Social Security benefit payments by about $43 per month. This Part B premium increase was more than offset by the increase in Social Security benefits, and the hold-harmless provision was not applicable in 2012 for most beneficiaries. Similarly, the 2013 Social Security COLA of 1.7%[79] increased the average monthly Social Security benefit by about $21 per month,[80] which more than offset the $5 increase per month in standard Medicare premiums. Therefore, the hold-harmless provision will not be applicable to most beneficiaries in 2013.

Part B Premiums Over Time

Part B premium changes through time generally reflect the growth in total Part B expenditures, although the exact relationship between Part B expenditures covered by the Part B premium has been changed by statute at various points. (See **Appendix A**.) The Part B premium has risen from $3.00 in 1966 to $104.90 in 2013. (See **Figure 1**.) For comparison, during a similar time period, average annual Part B benefit costs per beneficiary have increased from about $101 in 1970 (about $8.42 per month) to a projected $5,222 per beneficiary (about $435 per month) in 2012.[81]

Prior to 2000, the Part B premium decreased from year to year twice: once from 1989 ($31.90) to 1990 ($28.60) as a result of the repeal of the Medicare Catastrophic Coverage Act of 1988 (P.L. 100-360), and once from 1995 ($46.10) to 1996 ($42.50) as a result of the transition from a premium as determined by a fixed dollar amount under the Omnibus Reconciliation Act of 1990 (P.L. 101-508) to 25% of costs as directed under the Omnibus Budget Reconciliation Act of 1993 (P.L. 103-66).

More recently, because of the absence of a Social Security COLA in 2010 and 2011, most beneficiaries were "held-harmless" and paid the 2009 premium of $96.40 per month during those years. The standard 2010 and 2011 premiums, paid by those who were not held harmless, were thus higher than they would have been had the hold harmless provision not been in effect. (See

---

[78] Most new enrollees in 2010 were eligible to be held harmless in the second year of no COLA, i.e., 2011; these individuals continued to pay the 2010 standard premium of $110.50 in 2011.

[79] Social Security Administration, "Cost-of-Living Adjustment (COLA) Information for 2013," http://www.socialsecurity.gov/cola/.

[80] SSA Fact Sheet, "2013 Social Security Changes," http://www.ssa.gov/pressoffice/factsheets/colafacts2013 htm.

[81] For additional information on Part B and total Medicare cost growth, see CRS Report R41436, *Medicare Financing*, by Patricia A. Davis. For data on recent growth in specific Part B benefits, see the 2013 Report of the Medicare Trustees, pp. 133-148, http://www.cms.gov/Research-Statistics-Data-and-Systems/Statistics-Trends-and-Reports/ReportsTrustFunds/Downloads/TR2013.pdf.

"Protection of Social Security Benefits from Increases in Medicare Part B Premiums" for additional detail.)

Figure 1. Monthly Medicare Part B Premiums
1966-2013

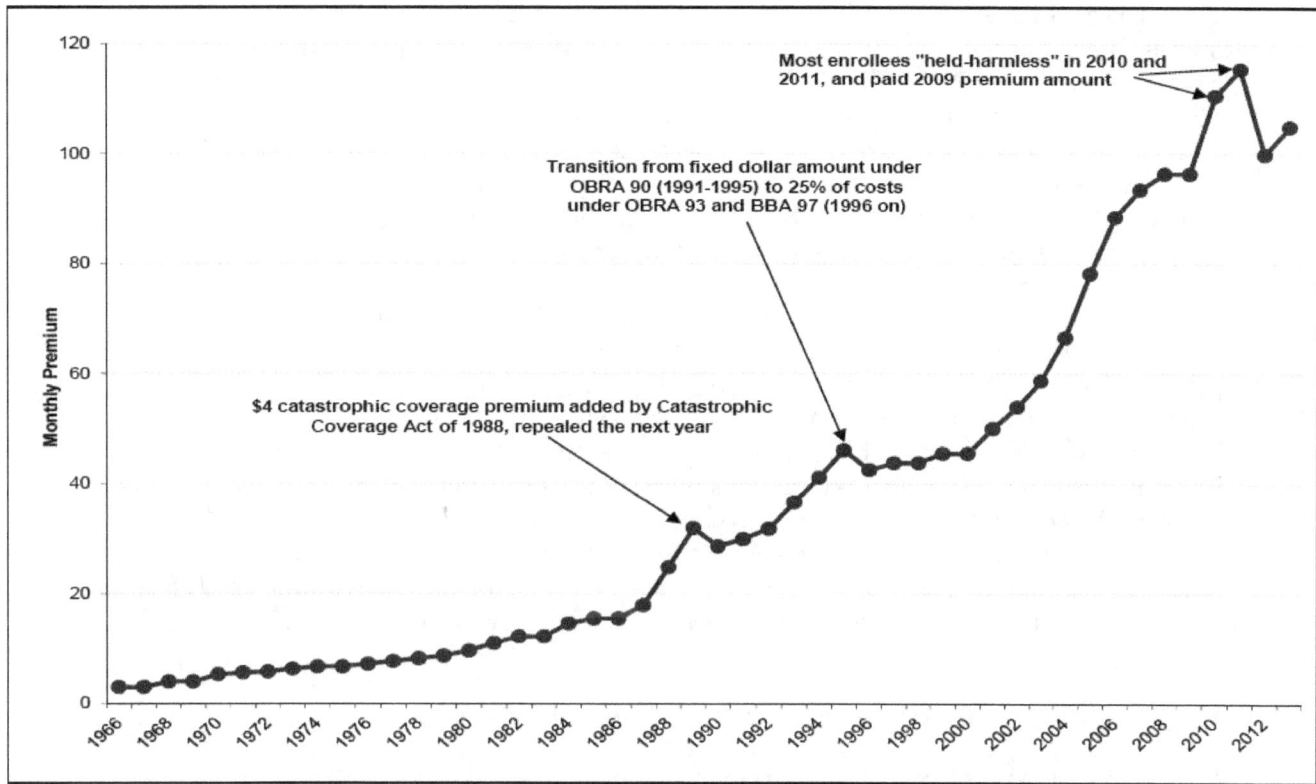

Source: CRS figure, based on the 2013 Annual Report of the Boards of Trustees of the Federal Hospital Insurance and Federal Supplemental Medical Insurance Trust Funds, Table V.E2 and Centers for Medicare & Medicaid Services, "Medicare Program: Medicare Part B Monthly Actuarial Rates, Premium Rate, and Annual Deductible Beginning January 1, 2013," 77 *Federal Register* 69850, November 21, 2012.

Since 2000, the Medicare Part B premium has more than doubled, increasing from $45.50 in 2000 to the current premium of $104.90 in 2013. Increases have been due to a number of factors that have increased per capita Part B expenditures during that time, including rising prices of health care services and equipment, new technologies, and increased utilization of Medicare Part B services. The CMS Office of the Actuary suggests that over the next 10 years, Part B premiums will increase more slowly than they have over the past decade, primarily due to ACA changes to Medicare payment methodologies that are expected to slow the rate of growth in spending for most Part B services.[82] Estimates of premiums in future years through 2022 may be found in **Appendix C.**

---

[82] The ACA did not make changes to the physician payment rate (SGR) formula. Solomon M. Mussey, CMS Office of the Actuary, Estimated Effects of the "Patient Protection and Affordable Care Act," as Amended, on the Year of Exhaustion for the Part A Trust Fund, Part B Premiums, and Part A and Part B Coinsurance Amounts, April 22, 2010, http://www.cms.gov/Research-Statistics-Data-and-Systems/Research/ActuarialStudies/downloads/PPACA_Medicare_2010-04-22.pdf.

Current Issues

Premium Amount and Annual Increases

The Medicare trustees estimate that over the next decade, Medicare Part B premiums will increase, on average, by over 5% each year. (See **Appendix C**.) Rising Medicare premiums could have a large effect on Social Security beneficiaries, particularly on those on those who rely on Social Security as their primary source of income. For example, among Americans aged 65 and older, 53% of married couples and 74% of unmarried persons receive more than half of their income from Social Security, and 23% of married couples and 46% of unmarried persons receive more than 90% of their income from Social Security.[83] Some of these beneficiaries may see a decline in their standard of living as their Medicare premiums rise.

Once a person has retired and elects to receive Social Security, his or her benefit is indexed to inflation and thereafter grows with annual Social Security COLAs.[84] However, Medicare premiums are based on the per capita cost growth of Part B benefits which reflect the growth in earnings of health care providers, and in the utilization and intensity of services used by beneficiaries, factors that have historically grown faster than CPI-U. This means that, over time, Medicare premiums represent a growing proportion of most beneficiaries' Social Security income.[85] Since 2000, Social Security's annual COLA has resulted in a cumulative benefit increase of about 36%, significantly less than the Part B premium growth of close to 120%. The Medicare trustees estimated that average Part B plus Part D premiums in 2013 would represent close to 11% of the average Social Security benefit, and increase to an estimated 19% in 2087.[86]

Proposals to Modify the Late Enrollment Penalty

Periodically, proposals have been offered to modify or eliminate the Part B premium penalty either for all enrollees or alternatively for a selected population group. Some have suggested modifying the penalty provision to limit both the amount and the duration of the surcharge, such as is the case for delayed Part A enrollment which has a maximum 10% surcharge, and a duration of twice the number of years that enrollment was delayed. (See **Appendix D** for information on the Part A premium and late enrollment penalty.)

Some have also suggested that Medicare Part B have a creditable coverage exemption, similar to that under Part D, that would allow Medicare beneficiaries with equivalent coverage to postpone enrollment in Part B without being subject be subject to a penalty. For example, under the Part D

---

[83] Social Security Basic Facts, http://www.ssa.gov/pressoffice/basicfact.htm.

[84] The COLA increases the benefits paid to *current* beneficiaries. In contrast, average Social Security benefits (those paid to new and current beneficiaries) have risen at a faster rate than the annual COLA, because the formula for calculating initial Social Security benefits is linked to *wage* growth, whereas the COLA is based on *price* growth. Generally, wages rise faster than prices.

[85] A "hold harmless" provision, described earlier, caps the annual Part B premium increase (but not the Part D increase) at the dollar amount of a beneficiary's COLA.

[86] Similarly, average cost-sharing was estimated to be about 12% of the Social Security benefit in 2013, and expected to increase to approximately 21% in 2087. *2013 Annual Report of the Boards of Trustees of the Federal Hospital Insurance and Federal Supplemental Medical Insurance Trust Funds*, pp. 41-42, http://www.cms.gov/Research-Statistics-Data-and-Systems/Statistics-Trends-and-Reports/ReportsTrustFunds/Downloads/TR2013.pdf.

prescription drug benefit, individuals are not subject to a late enrollment penalty if they have maintained "creditable" prescription drug coverage prior to enrollment, i.e., coverage that is expected to pay at least as much as Medicare's standard prescription drug coverage.[87] Creditable prescription drug coverage includes such things as employer-based prescription drug coverage; qualified State Pharmaceutical Assistance Programs (SPAPs); and military-related coverage (e.g., VA and TRICARE).[88]

In recent Congresses, several bills have been introduced to address the Part B late enrollment penalty. For example, H.R. 1654, introduced in the 112th Congress, would have established a special Medicare Part B enrollment period for individuals enrolled in COBRA (Consolidated Omnibus Budget Reconciliation Act) continuation coverage who elected not to enroll in Part B during their initial enrollment period. The legislation would have also created a continuous enrollment period that would have allowed Medicare eligible beneficiaries to sign up for Part B outside of the general enrollment period, and receive health coverage the following month. Additionally, the proposed legislation would have directed the Government Accountability Office to study problems with Part B enrollment. Also introduced in the 112th Congress, H.R. 103 would have, among other changes, eliminated late-enrollment penalties for those between the ages of 65 and 70. In the 111th Congress, H.R. 2235 would have limited the penalty for late Part B enrollment to 10% and twice the period of no enrollment, similar to the Part A late enrollment penalty. It would also have excluded periods of COBRA and retiree coverage from the penalty.

Proposals to Require a Part B Premium Surcharge for Beneficiaries in Medigap Plans with Near First-Dollar Coverage

In addition to the payment of Part B premiums, Medicare beneficiaries enrolled in Parts A and B (traditional Medicare) must also pay other out-of-pocket costs when they use services, such as deductibles, co-payments, and co-insurance. Because this cost-sharing can be substantial, and there is no "catastrophic" cap on out-of-pocket spending, most Medicare beneficiaries have some form of supplemental coverage, for example, through Medicaid or an employer. About 30% of beneficiaries enrolled in traditional Medicare buy Medigap policies from private insurance companies which cover some or all of Medicare's cost-sharing. Individuals who purchase Medigap must pay a monthly premium which is set by, and paid to, the insurance company selling the policy.[89] There are 10 standardized Medigap plans with varying levels of coverage. Two of the 10 standardized plans cover Parts A and B deductibles and coinsurance in full (i.e., offer "first-dollar" coverage). In 2010, over 60% of all beneficiaries who purchased Medigap insurance were covered by one of these two plans.

There is some concern that beneficiaries enrolled in Medigap plans with low-cost sharing requirements may have less incentive to consider the cost of health care services, and may thus increase costs to the Medicare program. Some have proposed imposing a Part B premium

---

[87] See Medicare publication "Your Guide to Medicare Prescription Drug Coverage," http://www.medicare.gov/Publications/Pubs/pdf/11109.pdf, p. 17.

[88] Employers or unions may also qualify for a federal subsidy to maintain prescription drug coverage for their retirees. Such subsidies are generally less expensive to the federal government than providing full coverage to such enrollees under Part D. *2013 Annual Report of the Boards of Trustees of the Federal Hospital Insurance and Federal Supplemental Medical Insurance Trust Funds*, http://www.cms.gov/Research-Statistics-Data-and-Systems/Statistics-Trends-and-Reports/ReportsTrustFunds/Downloads/TR2013.pdf, Tables II.B1 and IV.B10.

[89] See CRS Report R42745, *Medigap: A Primer*, by Carol Rapaport.

surcharge for Medicare beneficiaries who purchase certain types of Medigap plans. For example, the President's FY2014 budget proposal[90] would impose a Part B premium surcharge of approximately 15% of the average Medigap premium (about 30% of the Part B premium) for new Medicare beneficiaries who enroll in a near first-dollar Medigap plan.

Deficit Reduction

As Medicare currently represents about 13% of federal spending, most proposals to reduce federal deficits include suggestions to reduce Medicare program spending and/or increase program income. For example, some recent proposals would increase Medicare premiums as a portion of total program funding (i.e., decrease the amount of government subsidies).

Certain proposals would limit premium increases to high-income beneficiaries. For example, the President's FY2014 budget proposal would increase the applicable percentage of the program's cost per aged enrollee for higher income beneficiaries from the current 35% to 80% to between 40% and 90%. The proposal would also continue the ACA freeze on income thresholds until 25% of beneficiaries were subject to the high-income premiums.

Other proposals would increase premiums paid by all beneficiaries. For example, a proposal introduced by Senators Lieberman and Coburn[91] suggests raising the standard Part B premium from the current 25% of program costs to 35% over five years.

Finally, other proposals, such as that put forth in the FY2014 House Budget,[92] would place limits on the amount of the federal subsidy, and premiums would vary depending on the plan in which the beneficiary enrolled. In general, such "premium support" proposals would limit federal spending by changing the current Medicare program from a defined benefit to a defined contribution system.[93] Most such proposals limit the growth in the annual federal premium subsidy; for example, the House Budget proposal suggests a growth limit of GDP plus 0.5%. Depending on how such a proposal is designed, and should Medicare costs grow more quickly than the limit, beneficiary premiums could increase more rapidly than the amount of the premium subsidy.

Some of the issues that would need to be addressed when evaluating these types of proposals include (1) the ability of Medicare beneficiaries to absorb increased costs given their current levels of income and assets, as well as their other out-of-pocket expenditures (both health and non-health related); (2) the willingness of high-income beneficiaries to continue participating in Medicare Part B should their premiums continue to increase; and (3) the capacity of the Medicaid program to continue providing premium assistance to low-income beneficiaries should premiums increase.

---

[90] See CRS Report R43073, *Centers for Medicare & Medicaid Services: President's FY2014 Budget*, coordinated by Alison Mitchell.

[91] *A Bipartisan Plan to Save Medicare and Reduce Debt*, June 28, 2011, http://www.coburn.senate.gov/public// index.cfm?a=Files.Serve&File_id=1ea8e116-6d15-46ba-b2e0-731258583305.

[92] See CRS Report R43017, *Overview of Health Care Changes in the FY2014 Budget Proposal Offered by House Budget Committee Chairman Ryan*, by Patricia A. Davis, Alison Mitchell, and Bernadette Fernandez.

[93] Most premium support models combine Parts A and B benefits, and the premium subsidy and beneficiary premiums would apply to both of these parts of Medicare.

Appendix A. History of the Part B Premium Statutory Policy and Legislative Authority

The basis for determining the Part B premium amount has changed several times since the inception of the Medicare program, reflecting different legislative views of what share beneficiaries should bear as expenditures increased. When the Medicare program first went into effect in July 1966, the Part B monthly premium was set at a level to cover 50% of Part B program costs. Legislation enacted in 1972 limited the annual percentage increase in the premium to the same percentage by which Social Security benefits were adjusted for changes in the cost-of-living (i.e., COLAs). Under this formula, revenues from premiums soon dropped from 50% to below 25% of program costs because Part B program costs increased much faster than inflation as measured by the Consumer Price Index on which the Social Security COLA is based (**Table A-1**).

From the early 1980s, Congress regularly voted to set Part B premiums at a level to cover 25% of program costs, in effect overriding the COLA limitation. The 25% provisions first became effective January 1, 1984, with general revenues covering the remaining 75% of Part B program costs. Premiums increased in 1989 as a result of the Medicare Catastrophic Coverage Act of 1988 (P.L. 100-360), which added a catastrophic coverage premium to the Part B premium. The Act was repealed in November 1989, and the Part B premium for 1990 fell as a result.

Congress returned to the general approach of having premiums cover 25% of program costs in the Omnibus Budget Reconciliation Act of 1990 (OBRA 90, P.L. 101-508). However, OBRA 90 set specific dollar figures, rather than a percentage, in law for Part B premiums for the years 1991-1995. These dollar figures reflected CBO estimates of what 25% of program costs would be over the five-year period. However, program costs grew more slowly than anticipated, in part due to subsequent legislative changes and as a result, the 1995 premium of $46.10 actually represented 31.5% of Medicare Part B program costs.

The Omnibus Budget Reconciliation Act of 1993 (OBRA 93, P.L. 103-66) extended the policy of setting the Part B premium at a level to cover 25% of program costs for the years 1996-1998. As was the case prior to 1991, a percentage rather than a fixed dollar figure was used, which meant that the 1996 premium ($42.50) and the 1997 premium ($43.80) were lower than the 1995 premium ($46.10). BBA 97 permanently set the premium at 25% of program costs so that, generally speaking, premiums rise or fall with Part B program costs.[94]

The Medicare Prescription Drug, Improvement, and Modernization Act of 2003 (MMA, P.L. 108-173), as modified by the Deficit Reduction Act of 2005 (DRA, P.L. 109-171), required that beginning in 2007, higher-income beneficiaries pay higher Part B premiums.[95] The income thresholds used to determine eligibility for the high-income premium are to be adjusted each year

---

[94] BBA 97 made a change that had the effect of increasing the Part B premium over time. Prior to BBA 97, both Parts A and B of Medicare covered home health services. Payments were made under Part A, except for those few persons who had no Part A coverage. In order to extend the solvency of the Part A (hospital insurance) trust fund, BBA 97 gradually transferred coverage of some home health visits from Part A to Part B. Beginning January 1, 2003, Part A covers only post-institutional home health services for up to 100 visits, except for those persons with Part A coverage only who are covered without regard to the post-institutional limitation. Part B covers other home health services.

[95] MMA increased the Part B premium percentage for high-income enrollees; DRA accelerated the phase-in period for such premiums.

by the growth in the consumer price index.[96] The Patient Protection and Affordable Care Act (P.L. 111-148, Section 3402), however, froze these thresholds for the period of 2011 through 2019 at the 2010 levels.

Table A-1. Monthly Part B Premiums, 1966-2013

Year	Monthly premium	Effective date	Governing policy; legislative authority
1966	$3.00	7/66	Fixed dollar amount; Social Security Amendments (SSA) of 1965
1967	$3.00		Fixed dollar amount; SSA of 1965
1968	$4.00	4/68	Fixed dollar amount through March; Medicare Enrollment Act of 1967. Beginning April: 50% of costs; SSA of 1965
1969	$4.00		50% of costs; SSA of 1967
1970	$5.30	7/70	50% of costs; SSA of 1967
1971	$5.60	7/71	50% of costs; SSA of 1967
1972	$5.80	7/72	50% of costs; SSA of 1967
1973	$6.30	9/73	50% of costs; SSA of 1967 (COLA limit, added by SSA of 1972, could have applied, but was not needed). Limitations imposed by Economic Stabilization program set 7/73 amount at $5.80 and 8/73 amount at $6.10.
1974	$6.70	7/74	50% of costs; SSA of 1967 (COLA limit, added by SSA of 1972, could have applied, but was not needed)
1975	$6.70		Technical error in law prevented updating
1976	$7.20	7/76	COLA limit; SSA of 1972
1977	$7.70	7/77	COLA limit; SSA of 1972
1978	$8.20	7/78	COLA limit; SSA of 1972
1979	$8.70	7/79	COLA limit; SSA of 1972
1980	$9.60	7/80	COLA limit; SSA of 1972
1981	$11.00	7/81	COLA limit; SSA of 1972
1982	$12.20	7/82	COLA limit; SSA of 1972
1983	$12.20		Tax Equity and Fiscal Responsibility Act of 1982 (TEFRA) had set 25% rule for updates in 7/83 and 7/84. However, SSA of 1983 froze premiums 7/83-12/83 and changed future updates to January.
1984	$14.60	1/84	25% of costs; TEFRA, as amended by SSA of 1983
1985	$15.50	1/85	25% of costs; TEFRA, as amended by SSA of 1983
1986	$15.50	1/86	25% of costs; Deficit Reduction Act (DEFRA) of 1984
1987	$17.90	1/87	25% of costs; DEFRA of 1984
1988	$24.80	1/88	25% of costs, Consolidated Omnibus Budget Reconciliation Act of 1985
1989	$31.90	1/89	25% of costs, OBRA 87, plus $4 catastrophic coverage premium added by Medicare Catastrophic Coverage Act of 1988

---

[96] Social Security Act §1839(i)(5).

Year	Monthly premium	Effective date	Governing policy; legislative authority
1990	$28.60	1/90	25% of costs; OBRA 89. Medicare Catastrophic Coverage Repeal Act of 1989 repealed additional catastrophic coverage premium, effective 1/90
1991	$29.90	1/91	Fixed dollar amount; OBRA 90
1992	$31.80	1/92	Fixed dollar amount; OBRA 90
1993	$36.60	1/93	Fixed dollar amount; OBRA 90
1994	$41.10	1/94	Fixed dollar amount; OBRA 90
1995	$46.10	1/95	Fixed dollar amount; OBRA 90
1996	$42.50	1/96	25% of costs; OBRA 93
1997	$43.80	1/97	25% of costs; OBRA 93
1998	$43.80	1/98	25% of costs; OBRA 93 and BBA 97
1999	$45.50	1/99	25% of costs; BBA 97
2000	$45.50	1/00	25% of costs; BBA 97
2001	$50.00	1/01	25% of costs; BBA 97
2002	$54.00	1/02	25% of costs; BBA 97
2003	$58.70	1/03	25% of costs; BBA 97
2004	$66.60	1/04	25% of costs; BBA 97
2005	$78.20	1/05	25% of costs; BBA 97
2006	$88.50	1/06	25% of costs; BBA 97
2007	$93.50	1/07	25% of costs; BBA 97 (MMA and DRA authorize higher premiums for high-income enrollees: 1st year of 3-year phase-in)
2008	$96.40	1/08	25% of costs; BBA 97 (MMA and DRA authorize higher premiums for high-income enrollees: 2nd year of 3-year phase-in)
2009	$96.40	1/09	25% of costs; BBA 97 (MMA and DRA authorize higher premiums for high-income enrollees: 3rd year of 3-year phase-in)
2010	$110.50	1/10	25% of costs; BBA 97 (MMA and DRA authorize higher premiums for high-income enrollees, fully phased-in; hold-harmless provision applied to most enrollees who paid the 2009 rate of $96.40
2011	$115.40	1/11	25% of costs; BBA 97 (MMA and DRA authorize higher premiums for high-income enrollees, fully phased-in; ACA freezes income thresholds at 2010 levels from 2011 through 2019); hold-harmless provision applied to most enrollees who paid the 2009 rate of $96.40
2012	$99.90	1/12	25% of costs; BBA 97 (MMA and DRA authorize higher premiums for high-income enrollees, fully phased-in; ACA freezes income thresholds at 2010 levels from 2011 through 2019)
2013	$104.90	1/13	25% of costs; BBA 97 (MMA and DRA authorize higher premiums for high-income enrollees, fully phased-in; ACA freezes income thresholds at 2010 levels from 2011 through 2019)

Source: Various Annual Trustee Reports, including the 2013 Annual Report of the Board of Trustees of the Federal Hospital Insurance and Federal Supplementary Medical Insurance Trust Fund, May 2013; and Centers for Medicare & Medicaid Services, "Medicare Program: Medicare Part B Monthly Actuarial Rates, Premium Rate, and Annual Deductible Beginning January 1, 2013," 77 *Federal Register* 69850, November 21, 2012.

Appendix B. Standard and High-Income Part B Premiums and Income Thresholds: 2007-2013

Table B-1. Income Levels for Determining Medicare Part B Premium Adjustment and Per Person Premium Amounts

2007-2013 (in nominal dollars)

	2007	2008	2009	2010	2011	2012	2013
Standard Premium	Less than or equal to $80,000 *individual*	Less than or equal to $82,000 *individual*	Less than or equal to $85,000 *individual*	Less than or equal to $85,000 *individual*	Less than or equal to $85,000 *individual*	Less than or equal to $85,000 *individual*	Less than or equal to $85,000 *individual*
	Less than or equal to $160,000 *couple*	Less than or equal to $164,000 *couple*	Less than or equal to $170,000 *couple*	Less than or equal to $170,000 *couple*	Less than or equal to $170,000 *couple*	Less than or equal to $170,000 *couple*	Less than or equal to $170,000 *couple*
	$93.50	**$96.40**	**$96.40**a	**$110.50**b	**$115.40**b	**$99.90**	**$104.90**
Level 1	$80,001-$100,000 *individual*	$82,001-$102,000 *individual*	$85,001-$107,000 *individual*	$85,001-$107,000 *individual*	$85,001-$107,000 *individual*	$85,001-$107,000 *individual*	$85,001-$107,000 *individual*
	$160,001-$200,000 *couple*	$164,001-$204,000 *couple*	$170,001-$214,000 *couple*	$170,001-$214,000 *couple*	$170,001-$214,000 *couple*	$170,001-$214,000 *couple*	$170,001-$214,000 *couple*
	$105.80	**$122.20**	**$134.90**	**$154.70**	**$161.50**	**$139.90**	**$146.90**
Level 2	$100,001-$150,000 *individual*	$102,001-$153,000 *individual*	$107,001-$160,000 *individual*	$107,001-$160,000 *individual*	$107,001-$160,000 *individual*	$107,001-$160,000 *individual*	$107,001-$160,000 *individual*
	$200,001-$300,000 *couple*	$204,001-$306,000 *couple*	$214,001-$320,000 *couple*	$214,001-$320,000 *couple*	$214,001-$320,000 *couple*	$214,001-$320,000 *couple*	$214,001-$320,000 *couple*
	$124.40	**$160.90**	**$192.70**	**$221.00**	**$230.70**	**$199.80**	**$209.80**
Level 3	$150,001-$200,000 *individual*	$153,001-$205,000 *individual*	$160,001-$213,000 *individual*	$160,001-$214,000 *individual*	$160,001-$214,000 *individual*	$160,001-$214,000 *individual*	$160,001-$214,000 *individual*
	$300,001-$400,000 *couple*	$306,001-$410,000 *couple*	$320,001-$426,000 *couple*	$320,001-$428,000 *couple*	$320,001-$428,000 *couple*	$320,001-$428,000 *couple*	$320,001-$428,000 *couple*
	$142.90	**$199.70**	**$250.50**	**$287.30**	**$299.90**	**$259.70**	**$272.70**
Level 4	$200,000+ *individual*	$205,000+ *individual*	$213,000+ *individual*	$214,000+ *individual*	$214,000+ *individual*	$214,000+ *individual*	$214,000+ *individual*
	$400,000+ *couple*	$410,000+ *couple*	$426,000+ *couple*	$428,000+ *couple*	$428,000+ *couple*	$428,000+ *couple*	$428,000+ *couple*
	$161.40	**$238.40**	**$308.30**	**$353.60**	**$369.10**	**$319.70**	**$335.70**

Source: Centers for Medicare & Medicaid Services, Annual Notices, "Medicare Program; Medicare Part B Monthly Actuarial Rates, Premium Rate, and Annual Deductible," 2007 through 2012, and "Medicare Program: Medicare Part B Monthly Actuarial Rates, Premium Rate, and Annual Deductible Beginning January 1, 2013," 77 *Federal Register* 69850, November 21, 2012.

Note: When both are enrolled in Part B, each person in a couple pays the same individual premium amount.

a. The standard Part B premium in 2009 was the same as that in 2008; however, the lack of change was not due to the "hold harmless" provision. CMS determined that 2008 premiums and revenues were slightly higher than needed to cover costs in that year, and that 2009 financing would be adequate at the same premium level.

b. Due to no Social Security COLA in 2010 and 2011, most Part B enrollees were "held-harmless" and paid the 2009 standard monthly premium of $96.40.

Table B-2. Income Levels for Determining Part B Premium Adjustment for Married Beneficiaries Filing Separately and Associated Premiums

2007-2013 (in nominal dollars)

Income Level	2007	2008	2009	2010	2011	2012	2013
Standard	Less than or equal to $80,000	Less than or equal to $82,000	Less than or equal to $85,000	Less than or equal to $85,000	Less than or equal to $85,000	Less than or equal to $85,000	Less than or equal to $85,000
	$93.50	**$96.40**	**$96.40**	**$110.50**	**$115.40**	**$99.90**	**$104.90**
Lower adjustment category	Greater than $80,000 and less than or equal to $120,000	Greater than $82,000 and less than or equal to $123,000	Greater than $85,000 and less than or equal to $128,000	Greater than $85,000 and less than or equal to $129,000	Greater than $85,000 and less than or equal to $129,000	Greater than $85,000 and less than or equal to $129,000	Greater than $85,000 and less than or equal to $129,000
	$142.90	**$199.70**	**$250.50**	**$287.30**	**$299.90**	**$259.70**	**$272.70**
Higher adjustment category	Greater than $120,000	Greater than $123,000	Greater than $128,000	Greater than $129,000	Greater than $129,000	Greater than $129,000	Greater than $129,000
	$161.40	**$238.40**	**$308.30**	**$353.60**	**$369.10**	**$319.70**	**$335.70**

Source: Centers for Medicare & Medicaid Services, Annual Notices, "Medicare Program; Medicare Part B Monthly Actuarial Rates, Premium Rate, and Annual Deductible," 2007 through 2012, and "Medicare Program: Medicare Part B Monthly Actuarial Rates, Premium Rate, and Annual Deductible Beginning January 1, 2013," 77 *Federal Register* 69850, November 21, 2012.

Appendix C. Estimated Future Part B Premiums

Table C-1. Projected Part B Premiums

	Percentage of Program Costs Represented by Premium				
	25% (Standard)	35%	50%	65%	80%
2014	$104.90	$146.90	$209.80	$272.70	$335.70
2015	110.70	154.90	221.30	287.70	354.10
2016	115.40	161.60	230.80	300.00	369.30
2017	120.90	169.20	241.70	314.20	386.70
2018	127.40	178.30	254.70	331.10	407.50
2019	134.40	188.20	268.80	349.40	430.10
2020	141.80	198.50	283.60	368.70	453.80
2021	150.00	209.90	299.90	389.90	479.80
2022	160.50	224.70	321.00	417.30	513.60

Source: 2013 Report of the Medicare Trustees, Tables V.E2 and V.E3.

Notes: These figures only represent estimates of future premiums. Actual premiums are determined each year in the fall prior to the actual year the premium will be in effect. Additionally, these projections do not take into account legislation enacted subsequent to the issuance of the Trustees' report in May 2013 nor reflect economic assumptions that may have been updated since that time. The premiums above include an above-average contingency margin for the likely legislative override of the scheduled reduction in physician payment rates.

Appendix D. Part A Premiums

The vast majority of persons turning age 65 are automatically entitled to Medicare Part A based on their own or their spouse's work in covered employment. However, individuals age 65 and over who are not otherwise eligible for Medicare Part A benefits and certain disabled individuals who have exhausted other entitlement may voluntarily purchase Part A coverage.[97] In most cases, persons who voluntarily purchase Part A must also purchase Part B. The periods during which one can enroll are the same as those for Part B (see "Medicare Part B Eligibility and Enrollment").

The monthly Part A premium is equal to the full average per capita value of the Part A benefit ($441 per month in 2013). Persons who have at least 30 quarters of covered employment (or married to someone who has such coverage) pay a premium that is 45% less than the full Part A premium ($243 per month in 2013). CMS estimates that in 2013, about 604,000 individuals will voluntarily enroll in Part A by paying the full premium and about 50,000 will pay the reduced premium.[98]

Similar to Part B, a penalty is imposed for persons who delay Part A enrollment beyond their initial enrollment period (which is the same seven-month period applicable for enrollment in Part B).[99] However, both the amount of the penalty and the duration of the penalty are different than under Part B. Persons who delay Part A enrollment for at least 12 months beyond their initial enrollment period are subject to a 10% premium surcharge.[100] The surcharge is 10% regardless of the length of the delay. Further the surcharge only applies for a period equal to twice the number of years (i.e., 12-month periods) during which an individual delays enrollment. Thus, an individual who delays enrollment for three years under Part A would be subject to a 10% penalty for six years, whereas a person who delays enrollment for the same three-year period under Part B would be subject to a permanent 30% penalty.[101]

---

[97] An individual eligible to enroll must be a resident of the United States. Further, the individual must either be a citizen or an alien lawfully admitted for permanent residence who has resided in the United States continuously for the immediately preceding five years. Section 1818A of the Social Security Act provides for voluntary enrollment in Medicare Part A for certain disabled individuals who were entitled to coverage due to their receipt of disability benefits, but who have lost those benefits because they have returned to work and their incomes exceed the level of "substantial gainful activity." For additional information on Part A benefits for the disabled returning to work, see Social Security website "Working While Disabled," http://www.socialsecurity.gov/pubs/10095 html.

[98] "Medicare Program; Medicare Part A Premiums for CY 2013 for the Uninsured Aged and for Certain Disabled Individuals Who Have Exhausted Other Entitlement," 77 *Federal Register* 69859, November 21, 2012, http://www.gpo.gov/fdsys/pkg/FR-2012-11-21/pdf/2012-28274.pdf.

[99] The Consolidated Appropriations Act of 2001 (P.L. 106-554) exempts certain state and local retirees, retiring prior to January 1, 2002, from the Part A delayed enrollment penalty. These are groups of persons for whom the state or local government elects to pay the Part A delayed enrollment penalty for life. The amount of the penalty which would otherwise be assessed is to be reduced by an amount equal to the total amount of Medicare payroll taxes paid by the employee and the employer on behalf of the employee. The provision applies to premiums beginning January 2002.

[100] Similar to Part B, if one qualifies for and signs up during a special enrollment period, e.g., within 8 months of retiring, one may not be subject to a penalty.

[101] Prior to enactment of the Consolidated Omnibus Budget Reconciliation Act of 1985 (COBRA; P.L. 99-272), there was no upper limit on the amount of the Part A surcharge or duration of the surcharge. COBRA limited the amount of the Part A surcharge to 10% and the duration to twice the period of delayed enrollment.

Author Contact Information

Patricia A. Davis
Specialist in Health Care Financing
pdavis@crs.loc.gov, 7-7362

Acknowledgments

Jim Hahn and Jennifer O'Sullivan authored prior versions of this report. Barbara English also made contributions to this report.